From Control to Collaboration in Early Childhood Education

Classroom management is a popular topic in early childhood settings, but what exactly does it mean? In this eye-opening book, educators and caregivers are invited to redefine what it means to their teaching—shifting away from control and obedience and adopting a model of guidance, support, and celebration. Filled with reflective prompts and practical strategies, this book empowers early childhood educators and caregivers to create nurturing spaces that honor each child's individuality and potential. It shows readers step by step how to dismantle the outdated notions of management to foster a collaborative classroom environment where teachers and children partner in learning. With a welcoming, conversational style, *From Control to Collaboration in Early Childhood Education* invites you to rethink how you view children and your role in their educational experience so that we can cultivate classrooms that inspire joy, creativity, and a lifelong love of learning.

Samuel Broaden (he/they) is an early childhood advocate and author who believes in the power of childhood and showing children the power they have within themselves. He has worked in the early education field for 20 years—from teacher, to administrator, to quality coach, to author and speaker.

Other Eye on Education Books
Available from Routledge
(www.routledge.com/eyeoneducation)

Reimagining the Role of Teachers in Nature-Based Learning
Helping Children be Curious, Confident, and Caring
Rachel Larimore and Claire Warden

Promoting Language and Early Literacy Development
Practical Insights from a Parent Researcher
Pamela Beach

Teaching Higher-Order Thinking to Young Learners, K–3
How to Develop Sharp Minds for the Disinformation Age
Steffen Saifer

Everyday STEAM for the Early Childhood Classroom
Integrating the Arts into STEM Teaching
Margaret Loring Merrill

A New Vision for Early Childhood
Rethinking Our Relationships with Young Children
Noah Hichenberg

From Control to Collaboration in Early Childhood Education
Rethinking Classroom Management

Samuel Broaden

NEW YORK AND LONDON

Designed cover image: Shutterstock

First published 2025
by Routledge
605 Third Avenue, New York, NY 10158

and by Routledge
4 Park Square, Milton Park, Abingdon, Oxon, OX14 4RN

Routledge is an imprint of the Taylor & Francis Group, an informa business

© 2025 Taylor & Francis

The right of Samuel Broaden to be identified as author of this work has been asserted in accordance with sections 77 and 78 of the Copyright, Designs and Patents Act 1988.

All rights reserved. No part of this book may be reprinted or reproduced or utilised in any form or by any electronic, mechanical, or other means, now known or hereafter invented, including photocopying and recording, or in any information storage or retrieval system, without permission in writing from the publishers.

Trademark notice: Product or corporate names may be trademarks or registered trademarks, and are used only for identification and explanation without intent to infringe.

ISBN: 978-1-032-98865-8 (hbk)
ISBN: 978-1-032-98864-1 (pbk)
ISBN: 978-1-003-60105-0 (ebk)

DOI: 10.4324/9781003601050

Typeset in Palatino
by Apex CoVantage, LLC

For Perry, always.

Contents

Meet the Author viii
Land Acknowledgment ix
Introduction and Goals x
The Importance of Self-Reflection xiii
Our Goals xvii

1 **The Importance of Language** 1

2 **Dismantling "Management"** 10

3 **What Does "Classroom Management" Look Like?** 17

4 **The Solution—Classroom Collaboration and Why It Matters** 27

5 **Including Our Families in Collaboration** 36

6 **But What About . . . ?** 43

7 **Putting It All Together** 54

8 **The Importance of Giving Children Power** 61

9 **Final Reflections and Your Action Plan** 65

   Action Plan 68
   Discussion Questions 69
   Afterword 71
   References 74
   Acknowledgments 75

Meet the Author

Samuel Broaden (he/they) is an early childhood advocate and author who believes in the power of childhood and showing children the power they have within themselves. He has worked in the early education field for 20 years—from teacher, to administrator, to quality coach, to author and speaker. He believes in the importance of creating safe spaces for all children to discover who they are and be celebrated for that. He is the author of *Gender Expression and Inclusivity in Early Childhood: A Teacher's Guide to Queering the Classroom* and *Re-Thinking Weapon Play in Early Childhood: How to Encourage Imagination, Kindness, and Consent in Your Classroom.*

Land Acknowledgment

We acknowledge the land on which we sit and work in both Portland, Oregon and Austin, Texas (where this book was written) rests on traditional village sites of the Multnomah, Wasco, Cowlitz, Kathlamet, Clackamas, Bands of Chinook, Tualatin Kalapuya, Molalla, Alabama-Coushatta, Caddo, Carrizo/Comecrudo, Coahuiltecan, Comanche, Kickapoo, Lipan Apache, Tonkawa, and Ysleta Del Sur Pueblo and many other Indigenous peoples who made their homes here, creating communities and to live, create, and harvest and use the plentiful natural resources of the area. We take this opportunity to thank the original caretakers of this land and vow to do all we can to uplift and protect this land and the Indigenous peoples who did and still do occupy it.

Introduction and Goals

We hear so often in our work with young children that we need to have good "classroom management." There are many books dedicated to this topic, many so-called "toolkits" out there that promise to help us as teachers create classrooms of well-behaved and managed students. We may feel that by figuring out the secret to good classroom management, we can become the best teacher we can be. Our classroom may be celebrated for being so well-behaved. However, this should not be our goal. At all. What I am proposing in this book is that we completely do away with the term "classroom management" and everything that comes along with it—for good. We need to begin shifting our way of thinking from getting children to behave (which really means being compliant and obedient) to creating a community together with the children where everyone is respected, celebrated, and supported. Where their ideas, feelings, behaviors, emotions, and lives are valued and welcomed. Our job as early education practitioners is not to create classrooms of perfect children who do as they are told, never speak without being spoken to, or who are well-behaved. Our job is to create a space where all children are seen and supported; a space where we work together to create the experience we want; a space where we respect children for who they are. In order to do that, we need to shift our thought process from having good "classroom management" to having positive classroom collaboration.

Classroom collaboration (a term I am hoping will catch on and replace the dreaded other term!) is something that we can all do, if we begin to dismantle our previously held ideas of what our jobs are working with young children. It is something we can do once we begin to reflect on our experiences—both as children and as educators—to discover what it is we truly want for the children in our care. It is something we can do when we dedicate ourselves to offering children something different—something better. I am hopeful that this book and what is inside of it can help you on this journey. It is not an easy journey (nothing ever is when we are breaking up with long held ideas about childhood and education), but it is a journey that I am excited to guide you on.

My goal in this book is not to convince you that whatever way you are interacting with children or are running the classroom is the wrong way and that you need to throw it all away and do it my way. That is never my intention with anything that I talk about. My only goal through this whole process is that I can hopefully support you in thinking differently and just a little more deeply about your practice and the reason why you do the things you do. I hope to encourage you to reflect on your own practice and the experiences that you want the children in your care to have. I hope to encourage you to think deeply about the language that you use with the children and its connotations (both overt and under the surface), and understand how that language and those connotations may be informing the ways in which you interact with the children. By the end of this book, if you are thinking differently, thinking more deeply, and reflecting on your practice, then that is a win! Please understand as you read through this book that nothing I say is meant as an attack on anyone's practice—our job is already hard enough as it is, we don't need to feel shame for anything that we may be doing. (We will be discussing the cycle of shame with children later in this book as well). We are all in this together. This is something we can all work on continuously in our work—myself included. So don't feel bad if you read something and it makes you feel that you are not doing a good job—all I ask is that you reflect and think differently—think of the children first.

My journey to this was not an easy one. Like most of you, I was taught that having a well-behaved classroom meant that I was a good teacher. In fact, it was a selling point for my classroom. "Oh, you definitely want your children with Mr. Samuel, his kids are so well-behaved." It even got to the point where children who were "misbehaving" were sent to my room as a punishment because I had my children "under control." Now, I have to say that telling you all of this is actually quite hard for me and it makes me sick to my stomach that I was ever that teacher. But it is important for you to hear because we all are starting from somewhere and we only know what we know, and once we learn more, we can do better. There is no shame in being somewhere that you do not like in your practice and wanting to do better. The fact that you are reading this book is a sign that you are a good teacher—a great one even! Because you know there is something in our field that needs to shift. The disrespect for children and who they are as people needs to end. The control that adults feel they need to have over children needs to end. We can do that! We can begin to shift the ideas about childhood and children and what they are capable of and what they deserve. It is going to take work, but we are in this together! If you start to feel uncomfortable, good. If you start to get fearful, good. If you start to feel that shift within you, good. I will be here the whole way with you.

I believe in you. I am proud of you.

The Importance of Self-Reflection

Now, if you have followed my work at all or read any of my other books, you already know how ingrained the idea of self-reflection is in me and my work and how often I talk about it. That is because I truly feel that it is one of the best tools that we have as educators to create a better experience for the children and the families that we work with. Self-reflection allows us to dig deep into our lived experiences to see how those experiences may be informing who we are and how we interact with those around us. It allows us to notice and understand cycles and patterns, which is an invaluable resource when it comes to allowing us to make any changes we want or need in our lives. Reflection can also serve us well in our day to day life—not just in thinking about our past. We can use reflection in this way to ensure that we are on the right path for us and for our hopes and goals for our practice. How do we find that right path? How do we recognize and understand the goals we have for our practice? You guessed it—through reflection.

Here is how you can use self-reflection in both thinking about your past lived experiences and in your day to day life. First, *spend some time within yourself thinking and reflecting back to your childhood and your adolescence.* Think about the feelings you had, think about how the adults around you interacted with you, think about what level of support you did or did not have. Think about how the way you were treated or spoken to really made you feel. It is important during this reflection that we are 100% honest with ourselves. Sometimes when we are thinking about our childhood, there may be instances or experiences that we may not want to remember or look at with clear eyes—and that is understandable. However, in order to truly understand how our lived experiences have (and continue to) inform who we are and what we do, we need to be honest and work through these feelings.

Second, **I encourage you to think about your why**. This is a HUGE part of our reflection journey and a HUGE piece that will support us on this journey. Why did you feel called to work with children? Why did you want to work with children? Many times, this "why" can be connected to the self-reflection you've done on your childhood and your lived experiences; maybe you want to offer children a space or an experience that was not offered to you. Once you have thought about and discovered your why, write it down and place it somewhere that you will see it every day. (A Post-It on the mirror works great!)

Next, think about *what experience you want the children in your care to have with you*. How do you want them to feel? What do you want them to know? And I don't just mean in an academic sense; but more so what do you want them to know and understand about life, about themselves, about the world around them? This also connects to your own self-reflection of your experiences. (See how everything is connecting to each other? We will see this again and again as we move forward in this book.) This is a great thing to write down as well so that you can see it each day.

Lastly, you can use all of these things to support the reflection practices that you do every day. Each day as you are headed home or having some down time in the evening, think about your day. Think about the experiences you had, the words you said, the things that happened. Connect those things to your why and to *the experience you want the children* to have and decide if what happened today is aligned to that, and if not, what can you do going forward to work through that. Then you can use all of that reflection the next day to try to create something better. This can continue as you grow in your practice until it becomes a natural part of your day—and I promise you, you and your practice will be better for it. This also will allow you to connect with the children on a deeper level because if in your reflection at the end of the day, you recognize something you did or said that was not kind or positive, you can come back the next day, have a conversation with the children about that, apologize, and offer solutions for how you will work to be better. This type of interaction with an adult can be life-changing for the children as it can show them that they deserve an apology from anyone that has hurt them—even adults.

Here is an example of how we can put all those steps together in a self-reflection statement. I will use myself and my own reflections to share:

> As I reflect on my childhood experiences, I realize that there was a lot of support missing for me when it comes to my journey of self-discovery. I knew I was different, but I did not have support or any adults to look to that could help me understand what I was feeling or help me to understand that who I was was ok. Because of this, I decided that I wanted to work with children so that I could help to create spaces for them that I needed when I was younger, spaces where they feel safe, supported, loved, and important. That is the experience I want them to have while they are with me. I want them to feel powerful in themselves. I want them to know that they can be whoever they want to be. I want them to have a space where they are free to express and explore who they are. I want that experience to carry with them so that they can continue to grow and feel confident and powerful.

Did you see where each part of our self-reflection was in that example? Let's look again:

> *As I reflect on my childhood experiences, I realize that there was a lot of support missing for me when it comes to my journey of self-discovery. I knew I was different, but I did not have support or any adults to look to that could help me understand what I was feeling or help me to understand that who I was was ok.* **Because of this, I decided that I wanted to work with children so that I could help to create spaces for them that I needed when I was younger, spaces where they feel safe, supported, loved, and important.** *That is the experience I want them to have while they are with me. I want them to feel powerful in themselves. I want them*

to know that they can be whoever they want to be. I want them to have a space where they are free to express and explore who they are. I want that experience to carry with them so that they can continue to grow and feel confident and powerful.

There is going to be a ton of space and time in these pages to practice self-reflection. Like, I actually want you to write in this book! Mark it up! At times, it may feel uncomfortable or scary—but that is good! Push through that. By practicing self-reflection in your life and in your work, you can help to create a better experience for children—which is what we all want.

Use this space to begin to work on and create your own self-reflection statement. Actually write it here! Use the steps and example above to help you, but make it your own. And come back to this again and again! You can change it, you can update it—it is yours!

Reflections!

Our Goals

I always like to start all my trainings and workshops with some goals and I think that could also serve us well with this book. I feel that by setting goals for the journey that we are embarking on together, we can not only know where we are going, but we can also hold each other accountable as we move through this journey. Sometimes when we begin to shift away from more traditional ideas in our practice, it can be easy to fall back into old habits, back into the old familiar comfortability that we are used to. This is understandable for many reasons: first, breaking cycles is tough. Second, when we start to feel uncomfortable with something, we want to go back to what is known, safe, and comfortable. Third, our work is already hard and can feel lonely sometimes, but those feelings can begin to grow when we start to move and think differently. We can begin to feel even more alone in our practice when we start a journey like this. (Especially if we are working in a program where we are the only ones beginning to think differently!). But that is what is so special about this book and this journey we are taking—we are doing it TOGETHER! I will be here with you every step of the way and there are plenty of opportunities throughout this book for you to connect with others and gain support and encouragement.

So, let's get to these goals. The following are a few of my own goals for us during this journey. I have added space for you to write in any goals you may have for yourself in reading this book. (I would love to hear any goals that you have—more on how you can share those a bit later!).

Goal 1: I hope that we are all able to understand the importance of self-reflection and are able to use this tool to help us begin to dismantle the reasoning behind why we do what we do in our practice and our lives.

Goal 2: I hope that we can all come to this book with an open mind and also leave this book with an open mind—understanding that we are always learning and should always be open to hearing new thoughts, viewpoints, and ideas.

Goal 3: I hope that we can think more deeply and differently about the language that we use and what feelings and actions our words can create.

Goal 4: I hope that we are able to think of children differently than we currently do—with more respect, kindness, compassion, and honor.

Goal 5: I hope that we can move forward after reading this book and work together to create collaborative spaces for all children.

Are there any goals that you would add to this list?

Your Goals!

Now that we have decided on some goals for our time together, I want to let you know what you can expect as you continue on through this book. If you have seen me speak, or have read any of my other books, you know that reflection is a huge part of everything and this book is no different. So you can expect lots of space throughout the book for you to reflect and actually write in the book. Every chapter will have a space at the end for you to reflect on what you just read, and there may be other reflection spaces throughout the chapters if we talk about an especially important topic. I want this to be a guide that you can refer to over and over again as your practice continues to shift. I want this to be a book for you to take exactly what you need from it for your practice and I hope that you get whatever it is that you need right now out of it. If your copy of this book ends up looking dog-eared, marked-up with highlighter, written all in, and spine bent I will consider that to be a success. This book is not meant to be read once and placed back on your bookshelf forever—this book is meant to be carried along with you in your practice and in your journey, referred back to, and used to continually think differently in your work and in your life. So don't be afraid to make good use of it!

I also think that community is an integral piece of our work. Being able to connect with other like-minded educators who are working through similar journeys as ourselves is such a powerful feeling. That is why I created a community just for that—and I want you to be a part of it! You can find this community on Facebook by searching "Honoring Childhood the Community." You can join and connect with other educators who are reading this book as well and working through these shifts and changes right along with you. No matter if you decide to join or not, I encourage you to find your community. Find those around you who can support and encourage you in your practice. It will make a huge difference both in your work with children and in your life in general—it has been invaluable to me.

Are you ready? Grab a pen, turn the page, and let's get to work!

xx ◆ Our Goals

KINDLY,
Samuel

1

The Importance of Language

Language is an ever-changing idea. Merriam-Webster defines language as "the words, their pronunciation, and the methods of combining them used and understood by a community" (Merriam-Webster, 1994). As time goes on, words change, their meanings change, and what we use them for changes, and it is important that we recognize that and work hard to ensure that we are using appropriate, inclusive, and kind language. If we think back to our own childhoods, I am sure that there are many words or phrases that we could think of that are no longer appropriate—that is how language works. (Conversations with our grandparents or older generations of people can also remind us of outdated language sometimes, right?) We have a set of words that we use, then we learn more about those words, what they mean or how they make others feel, and the world around us, and we make shifts in that language to be more inclusive, kind, and respectful. One of the biggest examples I can think of when it comes to our field that I think is a perfect illustration of this idea is "criss-cross applesauce" (a way of children sitting cross-legged on the carpet), and the phrase that was used for that when I was a child which we now see as harmful to Indigenous communities, "Indian style." We would no longer use that phrase because we have since learned more about the world around us and have shifted our language to represent what we have learned. There are many other examples of this, both in our field and in our day to day lives. What examples of outdated language can you think of?

examples of outdated language?

There are also many aspects of language other than just the words themselves. You know this I am sure because you can tell in the way that someone says something to you what they may mean, and you can also tell if someone says the same thing in a different tone that it can mean something completely different. We see this all the time—think about those hilarious memes where it talks about someone from New York or somewhere saying the same phrase to mean ten different things—all depending on the tone.

You good= Are you ok?
You good= You are ok.
You good= How have you been
You good= Stop talking to me
You good= You're welcome
You good= No need to say sorry
You good= You need some money?
You good= Did you get enough?
You good = Do you have a problem?
You good = You bumped me?

Another important aspect of language to remember is that not only does all language mean something, but all language can carry a certain connotation with it as well that we may or may not fully understand. Here are some examples of what I mean:

LANGUAGE CONNOTATIONS

Confident ⟶ Arrogant

Curious ⟶ Nosy

Unique ⟶ Weird

Persuasive ⟶ Manipulative

You can see by looking at those examples that there can be a lot of meaning behind a word beyond just its definition and this is what I want us to be thinking about as we begin to discuss the ideas of classroom management and what we mean when we talk about shifting to a more collaborative space with children.

Fact: the language that we use with children matters. The language that we use when we talk *about* children matters. We know that children are looking to (and listening to) us to understand the world around them, to understand how people communicate and interact and to understand how they can fit into all of that. We are modeling for children each and every day in our words and in our actions—and this is a huge responsibility. Even when we do not think that the children are listening or paying attention to what we are saying, they are. Have you ever heard a group of children in your classroom playing "school" and you hear them pretending to be the teacher and you think to yourself "wow, that teacher sounds mean," and come to find out they are pretending to be you? Yeah, pretty eye-opening. (This has happened to me on numerous occasions, so don't feel too bad if it has happened to you as well.) But this illustrates the point perfectly—children are always taking in everything that we are putting out—positive or negative. So if we think about it that way, we can clearly see how important the language we use with them is.

Think back to your childhood for a moment. What language or words did adults use around you? What ideas were you taught through that language? Maybe you were taught to not speak up, maybe you were taught that you weren't good enough the way you were, maybe you were taught that your ideas or thoughts did not matter. All of those feelings can come from the language that is used. Take this for example: growing up I always knew that I was different from most of the other children around me but I did not know what that meant. However, the clues that I was given based on the language and conversations that were going on around me was that whatever it was that I was, it wasn't good. That is because all the things about me that I was noticing—my more effeminate ways, liking things that were "for girls"—were things that the men in my life were making fun of in others, or that they were using derogatory language toward other people who I felt were similar to me. So due to that exposure to that type of language, I grew up thinking that who I was was bad and that carried with me for quite some time as I began to grow and learn more about myself. (This is also a great example of that self-reflection I was talking about earlier!) So if we can understand that those examples are still carried with us now, we can understand that the language we use with children now will carry with them far beyond their time with us. That is an important thing to remember—so write it down!

What was placed in me as a child still lives within me, so what I place in children now, will live on within them.

Now, think about the language that you currently use with the children you work with. Is the language you are using with children language that you would have wanted used with you when you were a child? Is the language you are using with children now helping to create a different experience for them than you had? Is this language helping to support *what experience you want them to have with you*? Do you see or hear yourself repeating patterns of language from your childhood? It is important for us to be able to listen to ourselves and really hear ourselves when we speak so that we can understand how the language we are using is affecting the children. Use the graphic below to help you better understand the language you are using currently and help you reflect on any shifts that you could make.

LANGUAGE YOU USE CURRENTLY

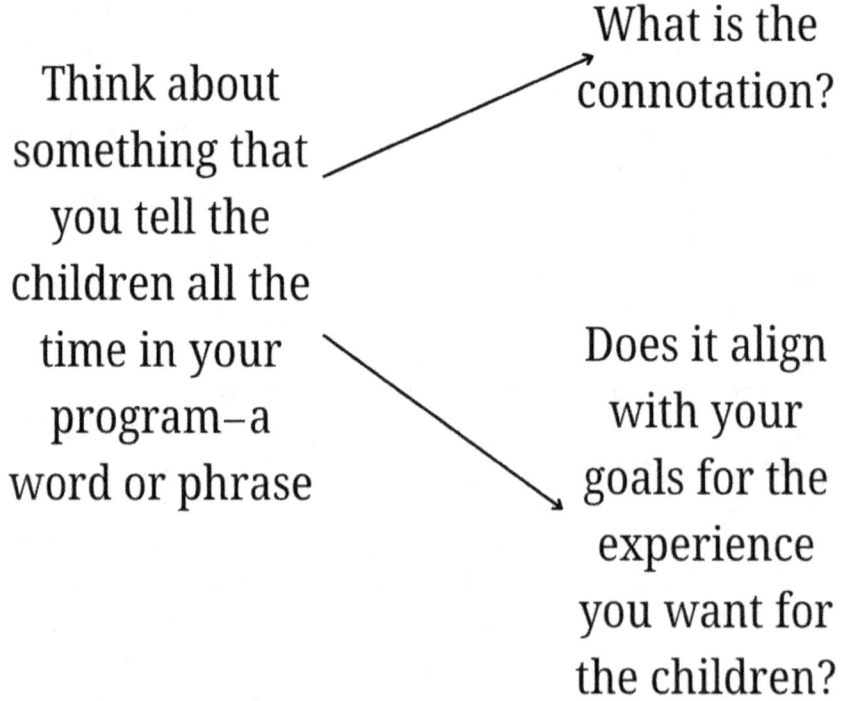

Ready for a little bit of a wakeup call when it comes to the language we use with children? So much of the language that we use with children can be based in control, shame, and our views of children as incapable people. That is a lot of what the field of education itself is grounded in at all levels when you think about it—control over children. We use language that devalues children, language that minimizes their feelings and thoughts, language that ignores who they may be. And so often, we are doing so without even realizing it. (I know I definitely have!) Let's take a look at some examples of what I mean and I want you to take notice if you use any of these words or phrases with your children.

"You don't know how to do that—stop"
"You are too old/young to do that."
"You're ok, stop crying"
"Boys will be boys"
"Don't be a baby."
"If you're a boy, line up first and girls will be next."
"Stop. Don't."
"Girls always have so much drama."
"Because I said so."
"No."
"Oh, he is here today so it'll be crazy."
"Say you're sorry."
"You're making me sad."

Did any of these bring any feelings up for you? Did you recognize any of these as things you may have said? Let me tell you something, I have said every single one of these at some point in my career. Does that make me a "bad" teacher? No! *Because we do the best with the information we know and when we learn more, we can do better.* Life is a journey and it is the same with our work with children. We should constantly be learning and growing. A lot of these words or phrases we say because that is how we were taught or those were the things that were said to us, right? Again, it is all about that cycle that we talked about. The words that were said to us, we tend to use. So growing up, most of us probably heard these words told to us a ton either by our parents, our families, or our teachers. And that is probably because those are the words that they heard growing up, and so on. Make sense?

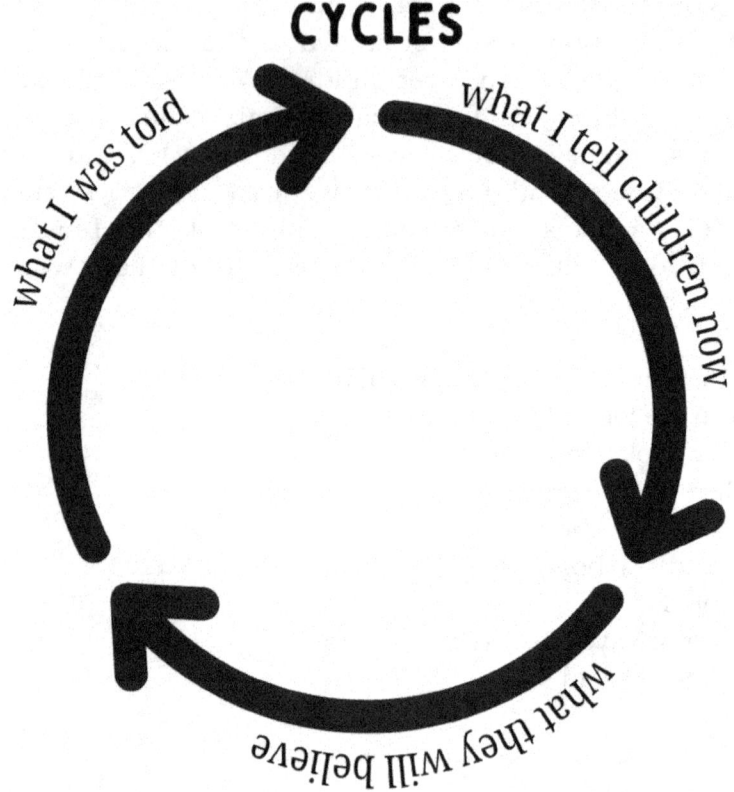

Everyone is doing the best they can with the information they have—but now, we are learning more so we can do better. We can stop the cycle of this type of language and create something better for our children. We can work to make these types of words or phrases a thing of the past that we would never consider saying (much like the criss-cross applesauce example). We can create a new cycle of positive language that uplifts children and supports them. We can think deeply about our experiences and what we were given as children and work to give something more to our children now. Now, I am not saying this is going to be easy so don't expect it to be. I cannot even tell you how many times a day, even now, that I stop myself when I use language that is not positive or kind and force myself to make the shift. Stopping cycles and creating new ones (especially when the cycle has been so ongoing and ingrained in almost all we do) is hard work and a lot of that work could end up bringing up memories, experiences, or times that we may have pushed to the very back of our minds; but it is important for us to take the time to do that work, to take the time to unpack and better understand our experiences and how those inform who we are today—both as educators and as individuals.

Also, you're amazing! And strong! And brave! And powerful! You can do this. Maybe those words were not words that were told to you growing up (or ever) but I am here to tell them to you now. You can do this. You can create a better experience for children. I believe in you and I hope you believe in yourself too. As a matter of fact, I want you to put this book down right now and I want you to say to yourself, "I am amazing. I am strong. I am brave. I am powerful." Yes, out loud.

Now, let's take what we learned about language and use that to think more deeply about "classroom management."

chapter reflections!

2

Dismantling "Management"

Now, what does all this talk about language and language shifts have to do with classroom management? How can we connect the two? Remember how we discussed the importance of the *connotation* of language? Well here is where we are going to put that all together. What do you think of when you hear the word "management"?

Reflections!

I think about work, a boss, telling people what to do, and controlling something. Do you think anything similar? Therein lies the issue that I see with "classroom management": **it creates an idea and a viewpoint in which we think we need to control children.** Now, the word "management" itself does not outright say that, right? It is the *connotation* that we should be concerned with and what that connotation can do to inform the way that we interact with children. If we use the term "classroom management," we could be taking the connotation of that word and using that to dictate how we work with the children. If we think about a boss, or control when we think of the word "management," we may inadvertently feel like that is what we need to do with children—and therein lies the issue.

Education in itself is rooted in control. In the idea that children need to be told what to do, what to say, and how to behave. Much of this is done through forcing children to sit a certain way, learn a certain way, and be a certain way—no matter what it is that they may want to do. I mean, that is always how it was for me growing up and I am sure for you as well. You sit at your desk, you do the work the teacher gives to you in the way they tell you to do it and that is it. You know, I used to be so proud to say that I was a "perfect student" as a child, it made me feel good knowing that I was a child who was doing so well in school. But now, I think—was I actually doing good in school or was I just doing exactly what the teacher told me to do without thinking or having my own mindset? That really opened my eyes to so much. I think that many of us in this field were the same type of student as children—we were the ones who always did our work, who did extra, who stayed after class to hang out with the teacher—so we may all have the same awakening when we realize maybe we weren't only good students, maybe we were that way out of fear of "being bad" or not being compliant. As much as we want to believe that education and the education system is here to help build students up and help them become successful, if we really dig down deeper and think about the true goals of education we can see that it is more about control than anything else. Let's break down some ways that we can see control taking a front seat in education. Feel free to add your own thoughts to this as well:

CONTROL IN SCHOOLS

In language

"No, you cannot do that."

In curriculum

"This is what you have to learn."

In bodily autonomy

"You cannot go to the bathroom now."

What I have found throughout my career and my own reflection is that education is more about preparing children to be workers in a capitalist society than about teaching them and helping them understand the world around them. Now I know that is a heavy statement but I really believe it is the truth. The system was created to discourage free thinking and creativity and instead encourage obedience, compliance, and "good behavior." We can see this when we look at different educational programs and schools and see what they offer children. We tend to see a lot of hierarchical thinking—where the teacher is at the top and the children are at the bottom. Where the teacher knows it all and it is the child's job to listen and take whatever the teacher says as fact. This way of thinking can lead to adults viewing children as less than and responding to them in that way. Now I am not saying that any of this is the fault of the teacher—this is the fault of the system that has been ingrained in us since we were children. When we were children, we were part of that system in school where we had to sit, do as we were told, and behave.

That is the idea that we got in our heads about what school was. We saw our teachers knowing everything, telling us how to do everything, and encouraging us to be "good"—so that is what we thought a teacher was. So it is not surprising to see that many of us grew up and brought those same ideas to our new roles in the education system—as the teachers. Again, it is the idea that we do the best with the knowledge and the experience that we have. But now it is time for us to think differently, gain new knowledge, and make a change in the way we do things.

Let's Dive Deeper

I want to take some time to dive a little deeper into what I mean when I talk about the education system being a preparation for being a member of a capitalist society because I feel that it is important to unpack. When we think about what it means to be a part of a capitalist society, we are talking about this idea of "eat or be eaten," right? A place where the wealthiest people in our society hold the most assets and the rest of us work for them. And often, becoming one of the wealthiest members of society is unattainable for the majority of us because of how deep rooted the wealth goes and the fact that those with money tend to stick with those with money and do not leave much room for any of us to break through. Therefore, most of us will end up being the workers. We end up spending most of life and most of our time working hard to just get by. I know I am not the only one who can understand that—especially in the world we are living in today.

One of the characteristics of a typical "worker" in this type of society is *silence*. We have been conditioned to believe that there is nothing we can do about our current situation and the only thing we can do to be successful in life is to continue to work and stay compliant out of fear that if we speak up or try to make a way for ourselves, that we will fail and put ourselves and our family at risk. So we continue to work our entire lives just so that we can survive while the wealthiest continue to gain more and more wealth. And we are ok with this because it has been what we've been taught since we were children. We are taught to sit and listen and behave so that we can be ready to sit and listen and behave (and work) when we are adults. And the cycle continues on and on until we decide to begin to unpack and rethink the way we do things. Now I know that to some this may sound like an exaggeration—how can the experience children are having in the education system be connected to our capitalist society? But it is connected. Education is something that every person will experience and that experience will inform how they grow and develop into adulthood. So knowing that, it is quite simple to make the connection between the control the education system has on its participants and the control our capitalist society has on us.

When we are thinking about *the type of experience that we want the children we are caring for to have*, I do not think that we want them to have an experience filled with adult control. I don't think we want them to have an experience like the one that is rooted in the typical education system. We want them to have something different, right? In order for us to give them a different experience, we have to do things differently. We cannot continue to feed the same system and expect different results. You know, a lot of times people will say things like "well, this is how we've always done it and it works out fine!" There are two things wrong with that argument—one, has it really worked out fine? And two, just because something has been done one way forever does not mean that it is the right way to do something or even the appropriate way to do something now. We need to start thinking differently about the work that we do and how we have the power to give children a different experience—one that is focused on them, their joys, their passions, their likes, who they are, etc. An easy way to begin to make this shift is to reflect on the language that we use when we talk about our programs and what we do with children.

We talked a little at the top of this chapter about the word "management" and what that word means and the ideas that it creates. If we are constantly thinking about our classrooms as things that need to be "managed," we are going to treat it as such. If we think about our children's behaviors as things that need to be "managed," we will continue to treat them as such. To manage something is to control it. If you are a manager at your job, you are controlling what happens there. If you are managing a classroom, you are controlling what happens there as well. We should not want to control our classrooms or our children. We should not want to manage them. However, by using this language so widely in our practice, we are subconsciously creating that type of environment. The more and more that we use a word to describe something that we are doing, the more we are going to respond in a way that connects to that word. Just the same way that if you hear your entire life that you are not good enough and will never amount to anything, you internalize that and may react in a way that matches with that statement. You may start to feel that you are not good enough and you may not feel encouraged to take chances in your life to better it; you may feel stuck in the situation you are in because you don't think you can do (or deserve) any better. We need to start understanding how the words and language that we use can inform the way we interact with children and the way we work in our practice.

It can be difficult to do this, especially when terms like "classroom management" and "behavior management" have been used for so long in our field. I remember I used to be so proud to have the best classroom management in my program—like that was a trophy or a badge of honor. I think I may have actually won a couple awards at the end of the year for the best classroom management—wow. Now I know that only meant that I had controlled the children in that classroom enough that they were the most "well-behaved" class. That is not what I want for my classroom anymore. But so many of us have been in the same situation—where we feel that having a classroom of children who listen and a classroom that is well-managed is the pinnacle of our work. I am here to tell you that it isn't. Our goal should not be to have a classroom of children who sit perfectly still and do exactly as they're told. Our goal should be to have a classroom of children who are strong, confident, and powerful, who feel connected to the people around them and feel that they are a part of something. We will discuss in a later chapter what that looks like in practice and how we can create that, but first I want to dive deeper into what a classroom looks like when "classroom management" is being used.

chapter reflections!

3

What Does "Classroom Management" Look Like?

Part of making a shift in our practice is taking a look at some things that we may currently be doing to see how those things may or may not line up with *the experience that we want the children to have*. We cannot expect to be able to make any changes in what we do if we cannot recognize the things that we may be doing that need change. This reflection is not meant to be a criticism of anything that you may be doing currently in your program—this is meant to be a way to help support you in looking at what you are doing in a different way.

> *Remember: We are all doing the best we can with the knowledge we have.*

When we look at a typical or traditional early childhood program, we can see many ways in which control of the children is happening a majority of the time. This may even include ways that we had not previously thought about or that we wouldn't think of as control. As you take a look at the following examples, I want you to reflect on your own program and if you notice anything in these examples that you may be doing in your program. Please remember—this is not a criticism of you as a teacher if you find yourself doing some of the things you see in these examples (I've done almost—if not all—of them myself!); this is a space for you to reflect and think more deeply about what you are doing. If you find yourself getting a little uncomfortable or find yourself feeling like you need to defend what you are doing in your program, refer back to my reminder and remember that we are all in this together to create the best possible spaces for children that we can. This can come with a lot of discomfort and anxiety as we begin to look beyond what we have been doing and work to make changes.

Examples of Control in a Typical Early Childhood Program

The first example that we often see in many traditional early childhood programs is what we first see when we walk in—the design and decor of the classroom. Now, this is not something that we may automatically think of when we think of control or collaboration with children, but it is a great place to start. The children should be having a say in everything that happens in the classroom—this includes what it looks like, what it sounds like, what it feels like, what it smells like, all of it. Oftentimes, when we think about our classrooms, we tend to think of them as "mine," right? How many times a day do we say "my classroom"? I know that I have said it more times than I can count. The important thing to remember is that the classroom does not belong to us alone. The classroom really belongs to the children. I am sure that we have all experienced a teacher leaving in the middle of the year (or maybe we have been the teacher to leave); when that teacher leaves the program, does the classroom go with them? No. So the classroom does not belong only to us, it belongs to the children and we share it with them. With this being the case, we should be including the children in all aspects of what makes up the classroom. We should be talking with them about what they want to put in the classroom, how they want it to look, if there are things they want to bring or make to add to it. When we walk into a classroom, we should be able to see that it is the children's space. However, we often see an adult-curated space with adult-made bulletin boards, adult-chosen decor, and little of who the children really are. How often do we get excited at the beginning of the year to go shopping for all the things we want to decorate our classroom with without even the thought of involving the children? Remember, we can and should be involving the children in everything we do in the classroom, so don't be afraid to have conversations with them and ask their opinion!

The next example we often see in traditional programs of control over collaboration is in the curriculum and the activities the children do. This can be a major culprit of control in the classroom because oftentimes, the curriculum that we use has very little space for the children to voice an opinion or have a say in what they do. I remember when I first started teaching, the first curriculum I used was a boxed curriculum that literally gave me a script for what to say to the children and when. I know now that that was, and is, such a controlling way to teach the children and did not give them any space or time to think for themselves. That is the issue with so many different curriculum programs—they are very adult-driven and adult-directed. They don't encourage creativity, flexibility, or children's choice. Yes, they may technically hit any milestones or stages that the children "need" to hit based on licensing or any other standards you may use, but if the children have no say in how they are learning those milestones or what they are doing in the class, how exciting or powerful do we think those learning times will be? We should want the children to be excited about what they are learning. Think about this in terms of yourself—if someone is teaching you something that you have no interest in or no excitement about, how much of that information are you going to retain or want to use going forward? On the other hand, if someone is teaching you about something that you are interested in and that you want to know more about, you probably will have a better chance of retaining that information and using it again. It is important that we work (no matter what curriculum we are using) to add the children's say and ideas into it as much as possible. One of the biggest challenges with this is that we simply may not have a say at all in what curriculum our program uses; we may just be given the box of curriculum and be expected to make it happen. Believe me, I know exactly how that feels! But there are still ways that we can create more collaboration with the children even with an adult-heavy curriculum, I promise!

Another example that we may see in a more traditional program when it comes to control of the children could be in their play. Now we all know that children learn best through play—but did you know that there is a huge difference in types of play? When we are talking about play that is best for the children, we are talking about uninterrupted, child-led play. That type of play is not as prevalent in programs as it could be. This type of play oftentimes goes against a lot of what we were taught to do with children or what is expected of us. I remember being taught that I should be instigating conversations with the children during their play to enhance their play and help them think critically about what they are doing. I was told to get on the floor and insert myself into their play so that they could learn more. However, when we look at true child-led play, the teacher should not be interrupting the play at all. True child-led play is all in the hands of the child. They choose where to play, what to play with, how to play, who to play with—all of it. Our job as the teacher is to support this play by letting it happen and giving space for it. I have to tell you, this was so hard for me, because I felt like if I was not inserting myself in the play that they would be missing out on learning opportunities and that if I wasn't there to control what they were playing or I wasn't there to steer their play in the direction I felt like it needed to go, that they would not be gaining anything from the play. It was so hard for me to shift away from interrupting their play to just letting them be, but it was such a power shift for my program when I did so. Now, this isn't to say of course that you should never be playing with the children—but let them come to you and invite you into their play. (Don't worry, this will happen!) Or just start playing on your own and they may come and join you. (We as adults often forget that play is for us too! We should be playing in life as well!) The point is—we should be encouraging the children to play as they want with no adult interference. Yes, they can take the blocks to the dramatic play area. Yes, they can dress up however they want. Yes, they can use all the paint and glue. No, they don't have to play with anyone. All of these things are ok. In fact, that is what true child-led play looks like.

Another way that we may see control being prevalent in a traditional program is in the schedule of the day. This is often something that is laid out very meticulously with everything during the day having a specific time and each thing during the day having a specific way to do it. This can sometimes lead to a lot of anxiety both for the children and for us. When we offer no flexibility in the schedule for the day and we move quickly in order to ensure that we are where we are supposed to be at the time we are supposed to be there, we can create a sense of urgency that is not needed. (Using my own reflection, I know that I have so much anxiety around being late and I am sure that comes in some part from the strict schedules I had to follow in school.) If circle time doesn't take 20 minutes or if we are 10 minutes late to lunch—it is ok. Everything will be fine. So often, we rush children, their ideas, and their play in order to make it on time to the next thing. Working with children is all about being flexible because not only is each child different, but each day is different too! Give yourself a little grace and just go with the flow! If the children are really into a certain activity, let it go for longer. Wouldn't you rather have them really be enjoying an activity than being rushed to end it and move onto something else? Nothing in our day is so important that it can't wait. Move with the children throughout the day. Collaborate with them on what you are doing, what is coming next, and how they are feeling about it all. Be flexible. Relax and breathe. I promise you once you begin to let go of that strict schedule, you all will feel much better.

As you can see there are so many ways throughout the day that we may be controlling children and what they do as opposed to collaborating with them on what they want their day to be like. Control doesn't just happen in planned activities or schedules for the day; it can also happen just in our conversations and the ways in which we interact with the children. When we ignore children's ideas or feelings ("you're fine stop crying"), when we tell them how they should or should not be feeling ("it is not that big of a deal"), when we don't respect them enough to have actual meaningful conversations with them ("that's nice, good job"), all of this is the opposite of collaboration. I want you to take a few minutes to reflect on some of the ways that we have seen control be a major part of a classroom and see if you can recognize yourself in any of those things. (Remember, it is ok if you do! That is the point of this book after all.) Think about other ways that you could be asserting control of the children instead of collaborating with them. Once you have reflected, turn the page and we will begin discussing some suggestions to combat each of the examples above.

Reflections!

Now that you have reflected a bit on your own practice and have noticed where there is room for more collaboration in your program, let's take a look at just a few suggestions for each of the above examples.

Examples of Collaboration

The first example we used was the way the classroom looks and how we create the physical environment of the room. Instead of focusing so much on this being "our classroom" and getting excited to go pick up things that we like to decorate, let's have a conversation with the children about what they want. Talk with them about what they want the room to look like: how do they want to decorate it, how do they want to display their art, what could we bring into the classroom that has a piece of all of us in it? These are great questions to start with in the conversation. Letting them know that you want to work together with them to create the classroom you all want to have is so important. Talk with them about how this is their classroom and they deserve to make it what they want. Talk with them about how they want it to feel in the classroom. Do they want a certain type of music or smell? Do they want to name the classroom something? Honestly, if you just start talking with them, the conversation will flow and you will find yourself working with the children in no time to create a classroom that is made by all of you.

The next example we talked about was the curriculum. Again, this can be a fairly difficult one to tackle, especially if we are working (like so many of us are) in a program that we do not own and in which we do not have much of a say in what curriculum we use. However, there are ways to still create collaboration with the children! In my entire career, I have only worked in one program that did not have a set curriculum for me to use, so I definitely understand this struggle. Here is a suggestion (and another instance of my favorite word making an appearance!): have a *conversation* with the children. Sometimes, just being honest with them can make such a difference. You can talk with them about how this is the curriculum that you need to use because that is what was given to you, but you want to make sure that the children are enjoying it and giving you their opinion on it. You could say something like, "This is what we are supposed to be learning about today, but I am curious if there is anything else you would like to learn or is there something about this topic that you are curious about?" This can not only help them to feel like they have a say in what they are learning, but it can also seriously enhance the given curriculum and you will be able to do more and teach them more than if you just followed the script. I mean, the people who write these curriculums may have knowledge of children or child development, but they don't know your classroom or your children, so enhance it with conversation! You can also use the skill of flexibility here to shift activities around or do an activity really quickly just to get it done and then move onto something that the children have spoken about being interested in. Look, I am all for finding a way around things and if the given activity is done, then what's the harm in doing something the children enjoy after?

Now let's talk about how we can create more collaboration in the children's play. Again, this one may seem simple but it can prove difficult (I know it did for me!). When we think about the children's play, the most important thing to think about is: are they leading their play? What I mean is, are they deciding what to play? Are they deciding how to play? Are they deciding when to play? Are they deciding who to play with? All of these things point to true child-led play and a collaborative approach to their play. So my suggestion is just back off! Seriously, just let them play and work on letting go of your own need to control the play or help them learn something from their play; because, guess what? They are already learning so much just by being in control of their own play. Make sure that they have adequate time for play and that play is as centered as you can make it in your day. Offer a variety of materials to explore within play (make sure they are open-ended materials!), and just let them go. They will learn so much and you will learn so much from them as you simply observe their play. It can be hard to let them play and just watch because that isn't exactly what a lot of us were taught, but you will see so much growth in the children when they play in their own way. So back up, let them take the lead, let them come to you, and let them play!

When it comes to strict schedules and the need to ensure that we are doing everything on time, this can be a difficult one to shift as well, especially, again, if we are in a program that we don't have as much say as we would like. Sometimes, we may be given a schedule of the day and we don't have an option to make changes to it. However, the skill of flexibility can really come in handy here. As can our ole' reliable: *conversation*. Just talk with the children. Let them know what is going on, let them know what the day looks like, ask them how they feel about it. If there are things they really feel like doing that day, make space for that. If you are doing an activity with them and they seem to not be into it, change it and do something else! I like to start my days by talking with the children about the day and what I was thinking we could do. Then I ask them for their ideas and if there is anything that they were really wanting to learn or do that day. Then, together, we create the day we want. If there are things that we just have to get done, we talk about that too and make space for it. These conversations not only can be great for children to feel like they are a part of something, but it can also be a good life lesson for them to understand that sometimes there are things that we might not want to do but we have to do them, and how we can work through that and be ok with that. When you are having honest and transparent conversations with children like this, your relationship with them will deepen and they will feel more connected to you and to the classroom.

Overall, one of the most important things that we can do to combat control in the classroom is have conversations with the children about what is going on. Even if we do not know what to say or how to say it, just be honest with them and work through it together. It is important to remember that this classroom belongs to all of us and it is our goal to create something that represents all of us and a space where we all feel heard and valuable. Shifting to classroom collaboration does not need to be a huge event with a ton of added stress and anxiety for you; it can start as simple as having the conversation.

chapter reflections!

4

The Solution—Classroom Collaboration and Why It Matters

As we discussed, there is so much control rooted in our educational system—from infancy all the way to college and beyond. It is our job as educators to think differently about our work and create something that is rooted in kindness, peace, and in seeing each person's value. It is our job to move away from control and move toward collaboration.

So what does collaboration mean when we are talking about early education? Honestly, it is a brand new way of viewing children—who they are and what they are capable of. For so long in our society, children have been viewed as lower class citizens, not even as whole people. They have been viewed as something that needs to be molded and created into the "right" kind of adult. They have not been respected for the people they are, for the ideas and thoughts they have, and for what they are capable of doing or thinking. Basically their thoughts, words, and feelings do not matter and we as adults are better than they are. We can see this if we reflect back onto our own childhoods again. What would have happened if you had told your parents "I don't like the way you are talking to me? It makes me feel sad"? Most likely, you would have been punished because that is seen as disrespect. Were you ever given the chance to speak about how you were feeling or what you were thinking? Were you ever given the chance to stand up for yourself? Were you even taught how to do that? Think about how your emotions and feelings were viewed by the adults around you. Think about how your likes, dislikes, fears, and passions were taken seriously or cared about. Most of the time, these things are not respected in children. If you speak up for yourself, it is disrespectful. If you don't like something, too bad you don't have a choice. If you are scared of something, get over it. If you are sad about something, stop crying. All of these are common for many of us to have gone through as children. It is important to think about how those experiences inform who we are now as adults. I will use myself as an example again. As an adult, it has sometimes been difficult for me to speak up for myself. It has been difficult to tell people when they have done things that have upset me and I have found myself to be a person who just aims to please, no matter the feelings that I am having or how it makes me feel. I have been someone who puts others before myself, many times to the detriment of myself and my emotions. Now, I have spent a great deal of time (and money in therapy!) trying to figure out why I am that way and so much of it—if not all of it—comes back to my childhood. I was never taught how to create boundaries for myself or how to advocate for myself. I was always taught to do what I was told and make others happy. So if I had no example of how to speak up for myself and I was always taught that speaking up for myself was a sign of disrespect, then how can I expect that as an adult I would do anything differently? Noticing this pattern is such a huge step in understanding how important the work that we do with children is because if we can recognize that our experiences as children have stayed with us and inform who we are as adults today, we can also recognize that the experience that we give children today will stay with them and inform who they are as adults. It is all about *what kind of experience we want to give to children.*

We know that so much of the experience of children now (and in the past) has been a product of control and the adult's need for power. It is a cycle that has just continued on and on, and we continue the pattern because that is all we know. It is the way that we experienced childhood, so it is the way that we give the experience to children now. But we can do better! We can do more for children now! So much of life, in my opinion, is working to make things better for those around us and for those who are coming after us. Just because I had a certain experience does not mean that others have to have the same experience. We hear that so often from adults—"well, this is what I had to do, so you can do it too!" Shouldn't we want something better for the next generation? The cycle can—and should—end with us.

So how can we move from control toward collaboration? First it begins with *reflection*. We need to spend time thinking deeply about our own views of children and of childhood. Do we view children as capable beings who deserve true respect and care? Or do we view children as things to be molded and controlled? That is the very first question we need to ask ourselves because that is where we are going to find the root of so much of our decisions and behaviors toward children. And it is important that we are honest with ourselves when we reflect and ask ourselves this question. If we just give an answer that we think is the right one ("of course I view children as capable beings who deserve true respect and care!"), then we cannot expect to make any true change. Remember, there is no right or wrong way to start this journey. If you have a belief that children should be told what to do and controlled in that way, that does not make you a bad person or teacher—it just means that with the knowledge and experience that you currently have, that is what you think. We are all learning and growing constantly. You may find that you cannot answer 100% one way or another. Most likely you may find that you fit a little into both ways of thinking—and that is ok too! Remember, we are coming out of a pattern that has been the same way for years and years—breaking cycles is hard! Once you have reflected and are able to decipher what it is that you believe about children, then you can begin the steps to shifting that perspective and breaking that cycle. Don't forget—reflection is an ongoing process. This should not be the only time that you reflect on your experiences or on your views about children. This is a starting point. You should continue this practice of self-reflection as you continue on in your practice to ensure that you are always doing what is right for children.

After we have reflected, we can begin to make some changes to the way that we view and interact with children on a daily basis. The biggest thing that I can tell you that will be life-changing in this process is *conversations*. Yes, my favorite word has made yet another appearance. But it really is the most simple and effective way to begin to shift the way we do things. As simple as it sounds though, it may prove to be a bit difficult for many of us. Can you guess why? Yup! Because it is something new that we have not had much experience with. We were never given the chance as children to have real conversations with adults and we were probably taught that as a teacher, conversation is more us talking at the children and getting them to understand something that we want them to understand. So it can be difficult to begin having actual meaningful conversations with children, and it can be uncomfortable. Believe me, the first few (dozen!) times I tried having these types of conversations with children, I was so awkward and so uncomfortable. I didn't know how to start, I didn't know what to say and I spent so much time feeling awkward that I made the conversation uncomfortable for everyone. So don't worry if it feels awkward to you at first or uncomfortable. Live in that feeling and just keep going. When we begin to peel away all the layers of what we think we are "supposed" to talk to children about and we just start talking to them, it will all become clear. You may also find that this can be difficult for the children as well because they most likely have not had many adults in their lives wanting to have real conversations with them where the adult was not trying to get them to do or say something or get them in trouble. This will be a learning process for all of us and that is ok! How can you combat that? Just start talking. It doesn't need to be something where we all sit down at circle time and talk about how we are going to be having conversations—just do it. Start talking to the children about your interests, about their interests, talk to them like you would talk to anyone else. This will start to build up that trust and connection and start getting the children used to expecting you—and other adults—to have conversations with them.

Having conversations with children can lead to many positive outcomes. First, you will be building a true connection with them and that is one of the most valuable things we can give them. Second, you will be showing them what they should be expecting from the adults and people around them. Children should expect respect and conversations and to be treated like an actual person. By doing this for them, you are teaching them what they deserve. You will also be able to work through so many of our daily issues with them in a much more positive, supportive, and kind way. Let's look a little deeper into each of these.

One of the most important things that we can do and give to children is that connection and trust. We want to build a trusting relationship with the children that we care for and we want them to feel safe and supported when they are with us. By having these conversations with children and breaking down this barrier between us (where the adult is at the top and the child is at the bottom), we can begin to build that deeper relationship with them. Speaking with children in a respectful way can be powerful for your relationship with them. So often, we see teachers speak to children in ways that devalue them. They are not at their level, they are using condescending or patronizing tones, or they are dismissive of their feelings. The types of conversations that we are talking about here are different and therefore more meaningful and powerful.

It is also important that we show children what they should be expecting from the people around them. By interacting with children with a barrier up between us, by interacting with them as if their feelings are not valid, and by interacting with them in a way that devalues them, we are teaching them (without even knowing it) that is what they should expect. So there is a chance that they will grow into adults who don't expect anything more out of the people in their lives, and the cycle continues. But we can teach them something different, we can teach them what to expect, we can teach them to set boundaries, we can teach them that they are worthy of all of these things—because they are. You have the power to give them something different that will help them to be stronger and more confident people; and that is pretty amazing.

Another really wonderful thing about having these types of conversations with children is that it can really help support us when things feel like they are going wrong. A lot of times when I talk about this subject, people will say things like "well, good luck with a bunch of disrespectful children who don't listen and don't behave because you let them do and say whatever they want." However, the opposite has proven to be true for me. By having conversations with children continuously, and by treating them with true respect, I have been able to better deal with situations that arise in our work—behaviors, family relationships, and more. Oftentimes, when we have a child with "behavioral issues," we are never collaborating with the child on how we can support them. We usually will collaborate with other adults to do what we think is best without ever actually talking to the child or figuring out what is really going on. By having conversations with children on a regular basis, we are building up the rapport and trust with the child, so then when they seem to be struggling, we can actually talk with them about what is going on and get to the root of what is happening and support them in a much more positive way than if we are not including them at all. *When children are given respect and trust, they are much more likely to reciprocate it.*

By having conversations with children on a daily basis, we can begin to collaborate with them on everything that is happening in the classroom. We can begin to include them in everything that is going on, and get their opinions and feedback to ensure that we are creating a space that speaks to them and that offers them exactly what they need. That is really the only thing you need to do to begin the process of shifting from control to collaboration. Reflect and have conversations. Then do it all again. Talk with the children about everything. Get their thoughts on everything. Remember, the classroom is not just yours—it is theirs too so treat it as such.

This idea can be used in any age group as well. Infants all the way to high school aged children deserve this type of experience. They deserve meaningful conversations about what is going on in their classrooms and during their day. The conversations may look different at different ages, but the underlying point is the same. We are treating all children with true respect and care. We are viewing all children as capable beings who deserve the same level of respect that we would offer to anyone else. So talk with the infants, tell them what is going on in their classroom, talk to them about what is going on that day. Talk with the toddlers and find out what they are excited about and wanting to learn more and do. All children deserve this. All children deserve collaboration.

Getting Rid of Rules

A really great example of collaborating with children on how our classroom will be comes from a personal experience of mine. I love telling stories because I feel that stories are such a great way that we can connect to each other. It also helps us to know each other better and better understand each other's experiences. A few years ago, I was teaching a Kindergarten class at a forest school. (If you know me at all, you know all about this class!) This year of teaching was a major turning point in my practice and really challenged me to think differently about so much of what I had been doing. One of the things that it made me rethink was the idea of classroom rules. I had always had classroom rules that were "written by the children," but really were just me leading the children into what I wanted the rules to be. In this classroom, I shifted my way of thinking and instead of creating a list of rules for the children that really didn't matter or have any connection to them, I decided to talk with them about what we wanted our classroom to be like and how we wanted to feel in the classroom. We then talked about what things we needed to do to make that type of a classroom. This conversation was great and ended with the creation of our classroom agreements. These were three agreements that we all agreed on and thought of together (for real this time!) These agreements were meant to guide us in all that we did in the classroom—yes, me included. These agreements were:

- ♦ we are kind to ourselves
- ♦ we are kind to others
- ♦ we are kind to the environment

Simple, easy to understand, and made with the children. We used these agreements the whole year to guide what we did. I used these agreements to help center myself when I wanted to say no to something they were doing. I would pause and think, "are they following the agreements?" and if they were, why was I saying no. Oftentimes, it was due to my own need for control or my desire to not deal with whatever they were doing; i.e., having to clean up all the paint or glue. This was such a great step for me in this idea of classroom collaboration and it made a huge difference in the way our classroom worked and how we connected and interacted with each other. We were also able to refer back to these agreements when our behavior maybe stepped outside the boundaries of these agreements. (Notice how I am saying "we"? That is because I considered myself just as much a part of these agreements as the children—we were in this together. Hence, collaboration!)

The Importance of Equity

When we are talking about anything that has to do with our classrooms or the ways in which we interact with children and families, it is imperative that we discuss equity, as so many of our children and families have been marginalized, ostracized, or otherwise excluded or treated unfairly. Through our work with children, we need to reflect and understand the ways in which institutionalized racism, white supremacy, and discriminatory practices have had an impact on the educational system and in what ways we may be contributing to that. We need to use this reflection to understand our privilege, if any, and what we need to do to advocate for and protect the children and families in our programs. This is work that we must do for ourselves and we cannot and should not expect marginalized people to explain or do the work for us.

chapter reflections!

5

Including Our Families in Collaboration

So often in our work, we are so focused on the children that we forget that a huge part of our work is our relationships with the families of the children in our programs. This is such an important part of what we do and it is important to consider how making the shift from control to collaboration in our program can connect to the families as well. Most of the time, the families in our program do not have education or experience working with children, so they do what they think is right based on their own childhood experiences or the things they see or read around them. We have already discussed how doing things in the same way that they were done when we were children can sometimes not lead to the best outcome, so this makes what we are doing even more important. The families are looking to us to help them understand their child's development and to help them better understand the best ways that they can support their child. This is such a huge honor and such a powerful position that we are in because we can not only change the experience that the children are having while they are with us, but we can also change the experience that the children are having in their homes as well. I say all the time that we may know the families and we may be friendly with them, but we never truly know what goes on when they leave us and go home. By connecting with the families through this shift from control to collaboration, we can hopefully create more supportive spaces for the children and their families at home too!

We already know that everything we do in the classroom, we should be involving the families. That is such an integral part of the home to school connection. But when we are beginning to make a shift in the way that we do things in the program, it is even more imperative that we connect with the families and support them through this as well. We can do this in the same way that we do with the children—through conversation. It is also important to remember that many of the families may have the same childhood experiences that we do and may also benefit from the same reflection practices that we did when it comes to their own thoughts and views on children in general and their own children. It could be beneficial to connect with the families in this way. By sharing with them your own journey of self-reflection and the things that you have learned and unlearned, it can empower them to do the same. Many adults may not have the space or the skills to embark on this type of self-reflection, but we might not at first either right?

It could be a good idea to either have a family meeting or send out an email or message to the families talking about some of the changes you are working through and how you feel it can benefit the children and how you want to support the families in doing the same. By creating this safe space for everyone to reflect, learn, and grow, we can build a stronger connection with the families in our program, which will in turn create stronger relationships with the children when they see the adults they care about in their life connecting with each other. Here is just an example of what you could send out to the families of your program to begin this process. Feel free to use this in any way that you see fit.

> Dear Families,
>
> I wanted to send a little message to let you know some things that I have been thinking about and reflecting on in our classroom and some changes I am going to be making in the way that we all work together in our program. I realized that for so many years, teaching has been about

control. When I think back on my own experience in school, I remember it being very rigid. I sat in an assigned seat, did my assigned work in the way the teacher told me to, and did not speak up or talk back. So much of what we do as adults is informed by the experiences that we had as children, and I think that so much of what I have been doing in the classroom has been informed by my experiences in school; I realized that I want to give something different to my students now. I want to work to create a space where the children feel like they are valued and have a say in what is going on in the classroom. I want them to feel like their words and voices are important and that I am really listening to them—what they like, what they don't like, how they want to be treated, etc. In short, I want to shift our classroom culture into a culture of collaboration. A space where I collaborate with them on everything we do in the classroom—from the decor of the classroom, to the activities that we do, to what they play. It is important to me to offer them this space so that they can hopefully go forward from this program feeling strong, confident, and powerful within themselves. They will still be learning all the same things, just in a way that is more in line with them and their interests. So going forward, I will be talking with the children about what it is they want, how they want their experience to be in the classroom, and what we can do together to make it happen.

  I am excited to embark on this journey with you and your children and I feel strongly that by creating a classroom culture of collaboration with the children that we will see a group of children who are strong, confident, happy, and kind. I also want to start doing more to collaborate and connect with you—I want to ensure that you feel like you have a seat at the table and that your voice and your thoughts are valid as well. The idea of a culture of collaboration includes you all too! So I will begin to brainstorm—with your help!—some different ways that you and I can collaborate as well. I want to open this classroom up to all of us and encourage you all to take part in it in whatever way feels right for you.

So much of this came about due to my own self-reflection on my lived experiences and the experience that I want the children to have with me. I encourage you to do some self-reflection as well about your lived experiences, your childhood, and the experience you want your children to have. It honestly changed so much of my outlook not just in the classroom, but in my life outside of the classroom as well.

If you have any questions, please do not hesitate to reach out to me. I am looking forward to creating a collaborative space with you and your children!

Whatever you decide to do to connect with the families in your program, it is important to ensure that they are a part of any shift that you are making in your classroom. We need to remember that it is our job to connect with and support the families just as much as the children—it is all connected.

We can also use this idea of collaboration when it comes to our work and our connections with the families as well. We can have conversations with them regarding what it is that they are hoping for their children to gain while they are with us—and also maybe what they themselves are hoping to learn as well during the time their children are with us. Oftentimes, families and parents may feel a certain level of disconnect from their child's school and teacher because in their minds and their experience, the teacher is the "end all be all" so to say in the classroom, so they may feel that they do not have a space or a place for input—but that simply is not true. Again, using our tool of self-reflection, we can let the families know that even though historically that has been the role of the teacher, we are trying to create something different here and we want (and value) their input and their voice.

Building a collaborative space for everyone is important. Ensuring that everyone involved in the classroom has a seat at the table—and knows that they have a seat at the table—is so valuable for the types of programs that we are wanting to create.

Here are just a few ways that you can accomplish this when it comes to the families in your program:

- Hold an orientation for the families before the school year starts (or before their child starts in your class) where you discuss how the classroom operates and how you view collaboration as a valuable piece of the classroom experience. This way they can understand what to expect going forward.
- Host a biweekly or monthly family meeting and invite all family members in to discuss what is going on in the classroom, at home, or anything that they may be concerned or have questions about.
- Create a classroom newsletter that offers not only information about the classroom but space for the families to participate in whatever way they wish. (Maybe you have a family member who is a chef and they want to share some recipes, etc.)
- Offer a "comment box" in your classroom where families can drop any questions or concerns or ideas they may have that they might not have the time to stop and talk to you about. This offers them the opportunity to have a say even if they don't have a lot of spare time to actually sit and talk with you.
- Invite family members into the classroom to observe, share, and teach alongside you. If you really get to know the families, you will start to learn their strengths or the things that they enjoy doing and you can invite them in to share those with the children.
- Create an online group that families can join to connect with you and with each other. They can post about play dates, ideas for the classroom, or just fun things that are happening at home.
- Ensure that the families have a way to stay connected with you—whether through an app your program uses, an email address specifically for your classroom, or any other communication that works for you. It is important for the families to feel like they have easy access to you (within boundaries of course).

What about if a family has an issue with you giving children the freedom to speak up and control their learning? Often, we may come across families that have the more traditional mindset of who children are and what they should be doing and they may feel uncomfortable with some of the things you do in your program when it comes to collaborating with the children. So how can we ensure that the family is comfortable and understands why we are doing what we are doing, while at the same time ensuring that the children have the type of space and experience that we want for them? I think this is why those conversations at the beginning of the year are so valuable. It lets the families know exactly what to expect and it also begins the process of creating a trusting and open relationship between the families and yourself so that down the line, if the family is feeling uncomfortable or unsure about what is going on, they will feel safe coming to you to discuss it and you can use that time to remind them of the previous conversations and also invite them to continue their own journey of self-reflection to better understand where their ideas about their child come from and what they can do to begin to shift those too. We want to make sure that we are not alienating any families due to their way of thinking or discomfort and that we are creating a space for everyone to feel comfortable speaking up and talking about their feelings. Collaboration is for everyone involved in the classroom—not just for you and the children.

These are just a few ideas that you can use to connect and collaborate with the families in your program, but don't let these ideas stop you from thinking of your own—or better yet, collaborating with the families to come up with something together! The important thing is to ensure that all the families feel that they are valued and that we want them to be a part of what we are doing in the classroom. We also want to make sure that we are encouraging interaction, connection, and collaboration between the families as well. Creating a true community with the children, their families, and you is a very important piece of creating a collaborative classroom culture.

chapter reflections!

6

But What About . . .?

Now, you may be reading this book and thinking to yourself, "well, we use our own program of classroom or behavior management in my program and it is good, so why should I make a shift?" Yes, there are many different management programs out there, there are many books and ways of thinking when it comes to classroom or behavior management—some that you might be using right now. I am not here to say that any one program or way of thinking is the right way or the wrong way—that is never my intention with anything I talk or write about. My only goal in all I do is to get you to think differently and more deeply about the work that you are doing.

With that being said, I think that it is important to discuss different management systems and strategies that are being used and use our tools of self-reflection that we have talked about throughout this book to think more critically about them.

One of the biggest and most widely used programs out there is the PBIS framework. (pbis) This is a framework that many programs use and it offers a framework for early childhood as well as elementary–high school programs. This is a program that I have used in programs before and it may be one that you have used as well. I want to reiterate that this book is in no way saying that one program is better than the other or that any program

DOI: 10.4324/9781003601050-6

is bad or should not be used. PBIS offers frameworks that are research-based and have many great qualities about them. They offer great resources for connecting with the families in the program and also take great care to ensure that equity is used in this framework—and all of those things are great! The program focuses on strong and meaningful relationships with children, engaging with families, and offering support for children who need it. Many other programs offer this same type of framework. We are seeing more and more strategies coming out to support "challenging behaviors" that are starting to focus more on the child themselves rather than the behavior only. And that is wonderful to see.

If you Google "early childhood classroom management," you will see many websites and articles that talk about effective strategies, proven tips, and more that promise to help teachers manage their classrooms effectively. As I looked through the first page of results, I saw pages and answers from huge organizations like NAEYC (The National Association for the Education of Young Children), different child care program apps like Brightwheel and Procare, and government sites. I was interested to see what these different programs had to say about classroom management and most of them had similar, if not the same, strategies. Creating routines, setting up the classroom, praise and encouragement, visual supports, and the materials in the classroom. All of those strategies are wonderful and definitely can help support a positive classroom experience. What I did find interesting and something that I think really connects with what we are talking about is the fact that all of those strategies are explained by the adults without any input or collaboration from the children.

Yes, creating purposeful routines is a positive thing for the classroom, but we should be creating those routines with the children. We can do this by talking with the children about what types of things we want to do during the day, in what order, etc. Of course, we can use our adult mind to help the children understand things like rest or quiet time can fit really well after lunch, but we should be involving the children as much as we can in the creation of these routines. That way, it isn't something that we are creating for them and telling them to do it. Yes, we know what we think works based on our experience, but each child and each class is different and encouraging the children to have a say in what goes on during the day can be a really powerful experience.

Yes, setting up the classroom in a positive flow can be important, but again, we can and should be doing this in collaboration with the children. We can use our adult mind once more to help the children understand things like putting all the shelves in one clump in the middle of the room probably isn't the best (I guess we could try though!), but this is another instance in which we can collaborate with the children. They will feel a sense of ownership over the classroom, they will feel more inclined to care for it, and they will feel a sense of pride because it is something that they have created, it is something that was made with their ideas in mind.

Yes, having materials and activities that are open-ended and meaningful can be a positive thing for the children and the classroom but this is yet another way in which we can be collaborating with the children. Encouraging them to have a say in what is in the classroom is very important.

So many of these things we automatically see as something that is the adult's responsibility. This is because, once again, that is most of our experiences when it comes to education and what a teacher is supposed to do. We should be creating the space for the children. We should be using what we know to make the space exactly what the children need. But how do we know what the children need if we don't ask them or talk to them about it? Of course we have more time on this earth and more experience than the children do and we can use that to give them new ideas or help them understand things, but there is absolutely no reason that we cannot or should not be collaborating with children in everything in our classrooms.

Another thing that I found interesting in reading through a few of these strategies from my search was that the goal of most of these strategies was to "keep children on track," "keep kids focused," "keep them behaving appropriately," and "directing their pent-up energy into planned lessons" (Procare, 2023). I hope that you can see where the language used in these strategies cannot be as positive or collaborative as we would like. Again, our goal should not be to get children to behave or get them to behave appropriately, it should be to create a space where they can be who they are. To create a space where they are valued, where they have a say, where they feel powerful and trusted. If we continue to focus on the goals of control—obedience, compliance, good behavior—we will continue to miss the most important goal of our work: creating a positive and supportive space for children.

Everything that we have been discussing in this book, all the ways in which we can be collaborating with children, you can still implement along with any other program you or your school may be using. This is not a standalone program—much like the idea itself, it is collaborative. You know when I think about my own philosophy on childhood and early education, I realize that it is not black and white—it is a mixture of so many different philosophies and experiences that I have taken the parts that speak to me the most and created a mash-up that is all my own. We can think about this in the same way. Many other programs for classroom or behavior management have great things about them that we can take and use along with our own ideas. So often in life, it feels like things need to be either this or that way—a very binary way of thinking, which simply is not true. If we begin to let go of this idea, we can open ourselves up to a new way of thinking and be able to take so many different ideas together and create something that works just right for us.

What I think is important to consider when we are looking at different strategies or programs is the language that they are using and the amount of collaboration with the children there is. These two are really paramount pieces in creating a collaborative space and it is important to have them in any "management" strategy you may be using—or thinking about using. We know that the language we use can inform the way that we interact with children, so if we see programs that use a lot of language that devalues children for who they are ("challenging," "issues," "negative," "dangerous," or any other language that labels a child by their behavior) we know that that may be a program or part of a program that we will not want to use. When we use language that devalues children or labels them based on their behavior, we can unintentionally create a bias toward that child that can inform the way we interact with and treat them. How often have you seen this happen in your own practice? Maybe there is a child who is known as the "out of control" child and when they show up, the teachers all sigh, or when they do not show up, the teachers are excited that they will be able to have a better day? Even that point of view can skew the way that we interact with the child and can cause us to not give them the same experience as the other children—or the experience that we want to give to all children.

It is also important to look at the amount of collaboration with the children these programs have. Many of the behavior or classroom management techniques that we see don't really collaborate with the children as much as take the adults' viewpoint on what is happening and make decisions based on that. But if we are not even having a conversation with the child about what is going on, how they are feeling, or what they are going through, how in the world can we expect to support them in the best way—for them? By having open, transparent, and vulnerable conversations with the children on an ongoing basis, we can create that sense of trust and belonging in them. That way when things arise that we feel need more support, instead of just assuming we know what is going on or assuming we know why the child is or isn't doing something, we can sit with them and have an open dialogue with them about it and possibly understand them and the behavior in a new a deeper way than before. This will also help the child to feel valued and cared for as opposed to feeling like they are just their behavior—"I am just the bad kid." This can help support us in looking at behavior through a different lens. We tend to look at behavior as something that the child is doing to us instead of something that the child is doing either unintentionally or to tell us something. You know we hear all the time that behavior is communication! That all behaviors are the children trying to tell us something. But that is not always the case. Some things the children do are things that they cannot control or understand due to some extenuating circumstances. This is why these conversations with them are so valuable! We can use these conversations to truly get to know the children, and in turn be able to support them in a more meaningful and powerful way.

If you are or are thinking about using any strategy or program to help support you with your classroom, I highly encourage you to dig deep into them and think about these things to ensure that what they represent aligns with your goals and the experience that you want for the children in your classroom. Remember, you can use collaboration in any program, but we want to be sure that the underlying ideas and what they represent are aligned with the ideas of treating children as capable beings who deserve respect.

Now, there are a lot of behavioral or classroom management tools that are not as positive as they could be and no matter how you look at them, there might not be a way to find something positive in them. These types of strategies usually include ideas that are punitive and designed to shame, embarrass, or otherwise devalue the child, their behavior, and their emotions. I have seen this most often when it comes to "behavioral guidance plans" or things of that nature. Many times, these "plans" are just a way for programs to document what is happening with the goal of removing the child from the program. The levels of expulsion from preschool programs is both alarming and disheartening. We see this overwhelmingly more with children of color. Between 2017 and 2018, Black preschoolers made up 18.2% of the total student enrollment, but made up 43.3% of out-of-school suspensions and 38% of expulsions (USAFacts, 2023). Also, during the 2017–2018 school year, preschoolers were disciplined close to 4,000 times and nearly 75% of those cases resulted in expulsion from the program (USAFacts, 2023). This is what we are talking about when we discuss the issue with "behavioral management" programs and strategies. Many of them do not view the children as actual people who need support from the adults as much as they view them as people to control and send away if their behavior does not align with the expectations of the adults; this is where we begin to see the preschool-to-prison pipeline forming. I am sure that you have experienced this at some level. How often have we heard that we just need to get rid of a child in our program because there is nothing we can do to make their behavior "better"? Here is the issue with this way of thinking: if a child does indeed need added support from the adults around them, pushing them out of program after program is not going to do anything for them but continue the cycle and make the child start to believe that there is something wrong with them. This level of discipline in early education is simply unacceptable and can be combated with the idea of classroom collaboration. We must start thinking differently about the ways in which we interact with the children in our programs and the ways in which we handle and deal with their behaviors. It is our job as educators to meet each child where they are and help support them through their growth and development. This is not going to look the same for every child; every child is not going to need the same amount of support from us, and every child is not going to be "easy" to support. Most often, the children who are going to need us the most are the children who are harder for us to support—for many reasons. Again, this is why our tool of self-reflection is so important. We have to spend time thinking about any biases that we may be bringing into our work that can prevent us from offering the support that each child needs. This can include biases based on our experiences, or based on what others have told us. Maybe we make an assumption about a child based on their family dynamic or the way the family communicates. Maybe we make an assumption about a child based on what others have told us about that child or that family. Those assumptions can inform the way that we interact with and support this child—whether we recognize it or not. That is why it is imperative that we spend time continuously reflecting and understanding any biases that we may come to the work with so that we can recognize those and work through them for the best interest of the child and their family. Here are just a few ways that we may be showing bias toward a child or their family:

- ♦ based on their race or ethnicity
- ♦ based on their family structure

- based on their visible or perceived disability
- based on their spoken language
- based on what others have said
- based on how they present themselves
- based on our feelings about their family
- based on their feelings toward us
- based on fear
- based on their behavior

Do you recognize any of these forms of bias as something that you have seen either from yourself or from someone that you have worked with? These are biases that many of us may have based on our own lived experiences and it is not a bad thing to begin to be honest with ourselves about them and begin to recognize the biases that we may have. So often, we correlate having a bias against a child or their family with us being "bad people," but that is not always the case. If we are able to honestly reflect and recognize any biases that we may have and earnestly work toward ridding ourselves of them so that we can support every child and family we serve, that is a good thing—that is growth and learning. However, if we continue to pretend that we do not hold any biases but still treat children or their families differently based on them—that is where we need to really consider what type of person and teacher we are. I encourage you to think deeply about your biases as you work through your self-reflection and I encourage you to be honest with yourself, because that is the only way that we can hope to do better for these children.

Oftentimes, when we begin to discuss any idea surrounding respecting children or thinking about children as equal beings, many people start to get upset or uncomfortable. I cannot tell you how many times I have had an adult tell me that I am teaching the children to be disrespectful by practicing this type of collaboration with them or that they are just going to grow up to be rude and have no respect for authority. Whenever we see a child who is behaving in a way that someone would typically describe as "bad," we hear people say things like "that's because these parents are too soft on them—they have no respect!" If

I had nickel for every time that I have heard that, we would all be millionaires! This is the type of thinking that we need to start pushing back against. Adults tend to have a preconceived idea of who children are and what they should be doing. This again, comes from their own experiences. ("If I ever talked like that to my mom, I would have gotten slapped, so don't you dare talk to me like that!") We need to dig a little deeper into those experiences and help others do the same. Often when we hear this type of thinking, it comes along with the phrase, "and I turned out fine!" I am challenging us to push back on that phrase with our own: "but are you fine?" Because most times, if we really think about it, we are not fine. If we really think about it, a lot of the experiences that we may have had as children could have really hurt us but we were never given the space to unpack that or even talk about it—so we push it down, we push it away and we think we are "fine." We are not fine, we are just ignoring the issue. But if all we do is ignore the issue, we will never be able to work through it—not just for the children, but for us as well. And I already know that you know exactly how we can begin to work through this. Say it with me—reflection! (I told you this would come up a lot!) That is the only way that we are going to be able to move forward and create a better life and experience for us and those around us. Now, again, it may be difficult. Opening up those old feelings that we have pushed aside can be uncomfortable and leave us feeling a bit lost. We don't really want to think about things in our past or our childhoods that were harmful. We don't want to think about our parents or other adults in our lives as doing something to hurt us. But here is the thing—in our reflection, we can also learn to give grace. We can offer grace in situations because we understand that we are all doing the best we can with the experience and information that we have. Life is all about cycles and the things that we experienced may be the same things that our parents experienced, and may be the same things that our grandparents experienced, so they do what they know. It is ok to reflect and understand that maybe some things happened that were not the most positive or conducive to our growth and development while at the same time understanding and recognizing that oftentimes, our parents were doing the best they could. Now obviously, we want to ensure that we are giving grace where it is appropriate and deserved, but oftentimes it can be. This includes giving grace to ourselves, don't forget!

So what do we do when we encounter people who balk at this idea of classroom collaboration or have an adverse reaction when we start talking about what true respect looks like for children? What do we do when we encounter people who say they already use a tried and true system for classroom management and don't want to think about anything new or different? It can be difficult, right? It can be hard to feel like we need to convince people of something. Especially if we are the only ones trying to convince. I have experienced that many times. We need to remember that we are advocates for children and that it is our job to not only do what is best for them, but also to stand up for them to ensure that they are being respected. This can be difficult, but it is something that we sign up for when we decide to work with children. Can you guess what my suggestion is going to be? Conversation and reflection, that's right. These two things can really make such a difference in everything that we do. So when you come across people who are uncomfortable with this idea (or any idea that you are trying to talk about), start with a conversation:

- ♦ start the conversation by setting a common goal; e.g., we all want to do what is best for the children and are willing to do whatever we can to offer them the best experience we can
- ♦ start explaining earnestly what you think and why you think it is best for the children; you can use examples from your experience or things you have read
- ♦ invite the other person's ideas and thoughts and be open to hearing them; you want to ensure that like the children and families, everyone feels like their thoughts are valued
- ♦ if the conversation starts to go off the deep end, you can pause and take a step back and remind each other of the goals that you set at the beginning of the conversation to ground each other back to what you are all wanting

- understand that making changes like this can take some time, but encourage the other person to embark on their own journey of self-reflection by sharing what it has done for you
- remind them that you are there for them as well and that you want to do whatever you can do to help support them in this journey as well

If you structure your conversation this way, you will have a much better chance of having a positive and meaningful conversation. Many times, when we are discussing things like this, it can be easy to get overwhelmed and begin to get angry or defensive, and that is not going to be conducive to any type of positive change. If the conversation is just not flowing or working in the moment, it is fine to take a step away and return to it at another point. No matter what happens, remember that it is your job to do what you think is best for the children—no matter if anyone thinks the same or not. You are the children's advocate—never forget that!

chapter reflections!

7

Putting It All Together

So, how do we make this all happen? We have talked about what it means to collaborate with children and families. We have talked about the importance of self-reflection in this process; and we have talked about why we should be wanting to make this shift from control to collaboration. But what does that actually look like in practice? Because it is one thing to talk about it and talk about why it is important, but so often we may have a difficult time actually putting it into practice. So let's talk about what classroom collaboration looks like from the moment you meet the children and families in your program through a whole day, through the entire time the children are with you in the classroom.

The Very Beginning

This can be one of the most important and valuable times that you have with the children and families in your program. This is the time that you can set those intentions for the year and really let the families in on what you believe and what they can expect out of the classroom that year. It is a good idea to have some sort of family meeting or orientation at the beginning of the year to spend time getting to know the children and their families, giving them time to get to know you, see the classroom, and hear about the way the classroom runs and what they and their children should be expecting. This is also an important thing to do for anyone new who comes into your program—not just at the beginning of the year. As children could possibly be joining your program at all times of the year, it is important that you offer this space to everyone. During this meeting or orientation, share with the families your philosophy and how it came to be. Share with them your journey through self-reflection and how that has helped you shape the classroom into what it is today. Encourage them to be collaborators with you this year and encourage them to connect with each other as well. Invite them to ask questions, voice any concerns they may have, and offer any suggestions they may have as well. By giving them this space to not only learn and hear from you, but also to offer their input, you are beginning the year (or your time with them if they are joining later in the year) on a note of collaboration and everyone will know what to expect from you and the classroom. This can be incredibly helpful also for when (and if) families have concerns throughout the year because by creating this type of relationship from the start, any other conversations that you have throughout the year can be much more positive and forward thinking than if you had not worked to create and cultivate this sense of collaboration.

A Day of Classroom Collaboration

So what does classroom collaboration look like during a typical classroom day? Or more importantly, what does it sound like? If you were to observe in a classroom that values collaboration over control, you would most likely hear many different conversations throughout the day—between the teacher and the children and between the children and each other. You will hear the teacher asking the children for their thoughts and opinions about what is going on throughout the day. Some things you may hear might be, "What are you wanting to do today?" "What do you think of this activity?" "How are you feeling about doing this?" "Is it ok if we move to a new activity?" "I want to know how you are feeling about what I just said," or "It is ok if you don't feel like doing this right now, is there something else you would like to do?" These types of questions show a true respect for the children's thoughts, ideas, and opinions. These types of questions also let children know the power they have in their words and that what they are or are not interested in is valuable in the classroom. You may also hear the children speaking up for themselves and for others. This may sound like the children telling the teacher "no," or explaining a boundary they have to another child. These are important things for them to be exploring because it is helping to build the foundation for these skills that they will need in the future—boundary setting, advocacy, and strength. The days in a classroom that values collaboration over control are filled with conversations, filled with questions, filled with curiosity. It is a space where questions and curiosity are encouraged and celebrated. Where children are encouraged to ask questions, to wonder why, and to challenge the teacher when they don't understand or agree. You may also see or hear a lot of different emotions happening, because in a classroom that values collaboration over control, all emotions are seen as valid and are encouraged to be felt and worked through. It doesn't give space for the silencing of children's feelings, it embraces them. The children are free to feel how they feel and are given the space to express, understand, and work through various emotions. You will see play! You will see the children exploring through various activities that they have created themselves. You will see the children moving from center to center, activity to activity, working together or alone to discover and play. You will see the teacher actively observing but not interrupting the play, but rather using the time to find ways that they can add, enhance, or shift different activities to meet the needs and interests of the children. You may even see the teacher participating in their own play or activities. You will hear the teacher talking the children through all aspects of the day—giving ample time and space for transitions, talking through tough situations, and building strong relationships with them. You will witness a classroom where children are respected, listened to, heard, believed, and valued. It might not always look or sound pretty, but it will look like a space where the teacher is actively working to engage the children in collaboration and a space where the children feel safe and supported.

Throughout the Year

A classroom that values collaboration over control will have various times throughout the year to reflect and make shifts in the way they are doing things. Remember, classroom collaboration is not a one-time experience. It is a living thing that will continue to shift and evolve throughout the year and years moving forward. It is important to take stock throughout the year of the classroom culture, use the tools of self-reflection, observation, and conversation to ensure that the classroom is a collaborative space, and make shifts or changes when needed. This can look different for each classroom but may include things like: monthly family meetings to discuss the classroom and collaborate together, mid-year check-ins with the children to ensure that they are feeling comfortable and like they are a meaningful part of the classroom, families coming in and supporting the classroom in various ways, or your own time in quiet self-reflection to ensure that what you are doing and the classroom you are guiding is aligned with your goals for the type of experience you want the children to have. These check-ins—with yourself, the children, and the families—are an invaluable tool to be sure that your classroom is continuing to value collaboration over control. It is also important because oftentimes, when we are making major shifts in our practice, if there comes a time when we start to get uncomfortable with the shifts, it can be easy to revert back to what is known and comfortable but if we continue to check in with ourselves (and with those who are supporting us), we can ensure that we are staying on the right track.

When it comes down to it, having a classroom that values collaboration over control relies on two ideas: reflection and conversation. If you get nothing from this entire book but those two ideas, you are golden. Being able to master the tools of self-reflection and conversation can change your practice in monumental ways. These tools can lead you to discover so many new parts of yourself—both as an educator and as a person—that you did not know before. These tools can help you to unpack, unlearn, and relearn so many things that can make your life better. But these tools work best when you use them continuously—not just once or twice. Reflection is an ongoing process; every day you should be reflecting on what went on during the day and see if that connects and feeds into the experience you want the children to have. Whenever you feel an emotion or discomfort come up, you should reflect on where that feeling is coming from and what you can do to move through it.

Don't worry if you struggle at first with these tools or with collaborating more with the children you work with. Remember, this is a learning process and it takes time. It takes time to dismantle old ideas and cycles and create new ones. Give yourself some grace. The fact that you are reading this book and wanting to learn more and do better for the children you work with shows what an amazing person and educator you are. So push through when you feel like it is too hard, and connect with those around you for support and encouragement. Talk with the children through these feelings. Most of all, remember that what you are doing is working to create a new and different experience for the children—one that truly values who they are as people and gives them the respect that they deserve.

What to Do if a Child Exhibits a Dangerous or Unkind Behavior

You may be thinking that all of this sounds great, but what happens when we have a child who is exhibiting frustrating, dangerous, or just unkind behavior. There is always going to be this type of behavior that adults find "wrong" in our classrooms because that is just how it is. Working with a large number of young children every day, we cannot expect for it to be perfect all the time—what is perfect anyway? We need to first reflect and understand our reasons for labeling behavior a certain way or why we think a certain behavior is "bad." Of course, these feelings can come from past experiences, etc. like all of our reflection, but it is important to recognize this because we may be reacting to a behavior in a way that is not positive based on our preconceived notions of what that behavior means or what we are willing to "deal with." We also need to understand that a child's behavior does not dictate who they are as people—we sometimes get that backward and that can lead to us labeling children based on their behavior like we discussed earlier. I don't think that you would want to be labeled based on your behavior, would you? So then why would we do that to children?

When we notice a behavior that we feel like could use a little extra support, the best thing that we can do first is to talk with the child and see if we can understand a little bit more about how they are feeling, what they may be experiencing, and how we can support them. This type of conversation steers away from any sort of blame or shame in the behavior and comes to the child fully ready to listen, understand, and support. This is made easier, of course, when we already have this type of trusting relationship with the child—which comes from this culture of collaboration that we've built. During this conversation, we want to make sure that the child understands that we are not wanting to get them in any sort of trouble, but that we really want to understand what they are going through and feeling—and that it is ok if they don't even know! Remember—children have been on this Earth for such a short time and are trying to navigate so many new emotions while at the same time being in a group of other children trying to do the same. It is a lot! Give them some grace and give them the respect of this type of conversation. During this conversation, you can offer solutions to help the child work through whatever it is they are feeling based on your own experiences. This can look like, "You know whenever I am feeling angry, it helps me to . . ." By giving the child examples from your own experience, you are showing them that the feelings and emotions that they are feeling are valid and ok to have—because we all have them! Another good thing to include in this conversation could be a reminder of the classroom agreements that you have all come up with together. This could look like, "I know you told me that you are angry and I saw that you took that anger out by hitting (child's name). I am just wondering how that aligns with our classroom agreements and if there is another way we can think of to work through our anger and still remain true to our agreements." There is no embarrassment or shame given for the feelings or even the behavior—because it is all natural. Instead the focus is on reflection, connection, and finding a solution together.

chapter reflections!

8

The Importance of Giving Children Power

One of the biggest things that children can gain from a classroom that values collaboration over control is a sense of their own power. This is such an important and valuable feeling for them to have and learn how to harness. When we are working through our own self-reflection, we may see that there were many times in our childhood when we were not given power or taught that we had any—not in our words, not in our emotions, and not in our boundaries. This may have led to us not feeling powerful in our lives now or as we were growing up. Maybe this caused us to enter into (and stay) in toxic relationships or friendships. Maybe this led to us being people pleasers and not being able to advocate for ourselves, our feelings, or what we needed from people. We should not want the same experience for the children we work with. Even though they are young, the experiences that they have with us now will in fact inform who they become as people—just as our experiences in childhood informed who we are now.

Some adults may be afraid of showing children the power they have within themselves—because they don't yet understand the power they have within themselves. This is an important piece to touch on. Many of us did not have the chance to understand the power we have within ourselves so now as adults, it can be difficult to know that and celebrate that power.

But that is what is so amazing about our work with children. Even though we want to teach children all these things and we want to be the ones they look up to—if we really think about it, they are teaching us so much as well! Our work with children (and the experiences that we are giving them) can be healing to our inner child, and by working through our own reflection, having conversations with children, showing them their power, etc., we can give those things to ourselves as well. I am telling you, I would not be the person I am today or be where I am today if I had not been working with children. I have been able to heal and learn so much about myself just by giving those things to the children. I have been able to recognize my own power by giving power to the children. I have been able to feel safe, strong, and confident in who I am by giving children spaces to find those things out for themselves. Care and education is healing work. It can really change your life. We are learning right alongside the children and when you see how knowing and understanding their power can make them feel and you see the difference in them, you will also realize, "wow, I can have that same feeling."

Don't be afraid to show children the power they have in their words, in their emotions, and in themselves. We want to raise and help create a new generation of people who are strong, and powerful, and confident, and who can think for themselves, advocate for themselves, and set healthy boundaries. This starts now, when they are with us. This starts with the experience that we give them now—that will carry with them for much longer than they are with us and for long after they leave our program.

Storytime

I told you that I love to tell stories, right? Well, I have one more for you that really speaks to this idea of showing children their power and how those experiences can stay with them. When I was a kindergarten teacher, I really worked to make the classroom one that was founded in collaboration and not control. We had conversations, children had a say, I encouraged them to advocate for themselves—all of it. The children would regularly say "no" to me, they would tell me what was upsetting them, they would tell me if I did something that did not feel kind to them. And it was an amazing experience. I felt so connected to those children and I knew that they felt seen, heard, believed, and trusted. Fast forward to a couple of years after that class moved on into public school. I had the mother of one of my students reach out to me to tell me that her daughter had gotten into trouble at school. This was odd to me because this child was just a joy. I asked the mom what happened and she said that the teacher said her child was disrespectful. I really could not believe that because that just was not this child at all so I asked what she did that was disrespectful. She told me that the teacher had said something to her daughter and the daughter had replied, "I did not like the way you said that to me, could you say that in a kinder way?"—and the teacher took that as disrespect. I was over the moon to hear this story because that is exactly the goal of classroom collaboration. That was exactly what I wanted the children to experience when they were with me. I wanted them to feel strong within themselves so that they could decide how they wanted to be treated and feel safe and confident enough to advocate for themselves if they felt that their boundaries were not being respected. That is how much what we show them now can stay with them because that child had been out of my classroom for about two years and she was still practicing what had been shown to her. It was amazing to hear and just encouraged me so much to know that this really is the way to do it. True collaboration means letting go of our own issues, letting go of our need to control, and showing children the power they have within themselves.

chapter reflections!

9
Final Reflections and Your Action Plan

Well, here we are. We have discussed a lot over the last few chapters. We have reflected, we have shared, we have thought deeply about the work that we do. I just want to take this opportunity to say thank you for joining me on this journey—I know change is not easy but I am so grateful that you are wanting to take steps to think more deeply about your practice.

As you saw, each chapter included a reflection piece at the end which I hope you were able to use to think about what was said in each chapter. My goal in this book is not to get you to agree with everything I say or get you to completely shift your practice tomorrow. My goal is, and always will be, to help you to think more deeply about the work that we do, about the reasons why we do it, about what it is we truly want for children, and how we can create the best possible space and experience for them.

Now that we are at the end of this book, I encourage you to spend some time in reflection on everything you read and all the feelings and thoughts that you may have had throughout. I have included some reflection prompts here to give you a little support if you are feeling stuck on what to reflect on.

♦ What surprised you the most as you were reading?

♦ When you picked up the book, what were you hoping to gain from it?

♦ How did you feel about your practice before you read this book? Were there things that you were wanting to shift?

♦ What feelings came up for you as you were reading? Was anything uncomfortable or triggering for you?

- How was the process of reflection for you? Was it easy? Difficult?

- What were your thoughts on "classroom management" before? Are they different now?

- Were you able to reflect on the language you use with the children? What shifts can you make?

- How prepared do you feel to advocate for children to people who think differently?

Action Plan

Use this space to create your action plan. Remember to reflect on what you have read and learned and use that reflection to create actionable steps that you can take to begin to create a classroom of collaboration with your students tomorrow. Feel free to share your action plan on our Facebook group to gain support, encouragement, and accountability.

Discussion Questions

Use the following questions to guide a discussion with your staff or your co-workers, book club, or anyone else!

1. What do you think of when you hear the words "classroom management"?

2. What do you consider to be a good classroom strategy?

3. What is the number one thing you want children to experience in your program?

4. Are there ways in which you exert control over the children in your program?

5. How important is it to connect with the families of those in your program? Why?

6. How do you view children?

7. What feelings came up for you as you read this book?

8. Have you made any shifts in your classroom from more traditional ideas?

9. What does collaboration in the classroom mean to you? What does it look like?

10. Are there any shifts that you feel like you want to make after reading this book?

11. How can you support other teachers through any shifts they are making?

Afterword

A Message for YOU!

I wanted to take some time to talk to you educator to educator and let you know that I see you! I know how hard the work is that you do each and every day. I know that you work so hard to create spaces and experiences for children that are positive, fun, and meaningful. I also know how much this job can wear on you. I know how much those feelings of anxiety, stress, thanklessness, despair, imposter syndrome, and more can impact your day and the work that you do. I know because I have been there myself—so many times. There were so many days that I would go home and just feel like giving up. Just feel like maybe this is not what I am supposed to be doing; I am not doing enough, I am not a good teacher, these children deserve better. It happens a lot more often than people may think. Everyone looks at the work that we do and thinks "wow you love kids so much, it must be so wonderful to work with them and you must be happy and joyful all the time!" when in reality it isn't always like that. And it can be hard to work through those feelings because you don't really understand them truly unless you have experienced them yourself. So even if you have a super supportive partner at home that you can vent to, sometimes you need someone who really understands how it feels.

Finding a community of people who understand what it is we go through as early educators is so important to our well-being. That is why I want to encourage you to join our community on Facebook! It is a group of like-minded educators who come together to support and encourage each other and it really is such a great space to connect. You can find it just by searching "Honoring Childhood the Community" on Facebook. We would love to have you.

Whatever you do, I encourage you to find that group of people who can understand your struggles, support and encourage you when you need it, and can build you up, because I truly do believe that it will make a huge difference in your practice and in your life.

I hope you know that what you do each day is valuable and important and that the children you work with each day are so lucky to have you.

I am here for you. I believe in you. You are doing a great job—don't you ever forget that!

A Letter from You to Your Younger Self

There is an exercise that I love doing that I think is really powerful and I think connects perfectly to this book, what we've talked about, and our own journey of self-reflection. This exercise is a letter to your younger self. Oftentimes, through our own self-reflection, we may realize things from our childhood that are uncomfortable, upsetting, or just otherwise not positive. Sometimes those things came from the adults in our lives and sometimes those things came from us and the way that we coped with what was going on in our lives. For example, maybe we did not let a certain part of ourselves out because we were worried about what others may think due to the messages that we may have received from the world around us. It can be a very powerful thing to take some time to compose a letter to your younger self and think about the things that you would want your younger self to know about life, your journey, and the things that you know now.

I encourage you to spend some time in reflection and spend some time writing this letter to your younger self. Use this letter as a space to not only reflect, but to offer grace, forgiveness, an apology, or strength to your younger self. Like I said before, the work that we do with children can be healing work for us as well, and for the child that still lives inside us all. So talk to the child that is inside you. Support them, encourage them, love them.

You know, one of our favorite shows in our house is *RuPaul's Drag Race*, and at the end of the competition, RuPaul holds up a picture of the finalists of the show as children and asks them what they would say to their younger selves. It is a very moving and emotional moment in the show and one that shows just how much those children that live inside of us still need from us. It is a moment in the show that is usually filled with tears and laughter as the contestants reminisce about their childhood and speak to their younger selves. This is what I am encouraging you to do now. Speak to your younger self, write to your younger self, forgive your younger self, offer grace. I really think that this could be a powerful moment for you (I know it was for me) and can really help you build that connection of *what experience you are wanting for the children in your care now*.

References

Center on PBIS. (n.d.). *Early childhood PBIS*. www.pbis.org/topics/early-childhood-pbis

Merriam-Webster. (1994). *Dictionary of English usage*. Merriam-Webster.

Procare. (2023, March 23). *12 classroom management strategies for preschool: Procare*. Procare Solutions. www.procaresoftware.com/blog/12-classroom-management-strategies-to-support-learning

USAFacts. (2023, March 23). *Black students are more likely to be punished than white students*. https://usafacts.org/articles/black-students-more-likely-to-be-punished-than-white-students/#:~:text=Preschool%20discipline,signing%20up%20for%20our%20newsletter

Acknowledgments

I truly hope that you gained something from this journey with me. I hope that you were able to think more deeply about yourself and your practice. I hope that you feel more confident and prepared to go forward and continue giving children the best you can. Please reach out to me and let's connect more on this idea. I love talking about all things childhood and I love gaining new connections and relationships with others who view childhood in this way as well. Thank you for joining me on this journey, I am so honored to have shared this space with you.

All I have wanted to do since I started working with children is to create a special place for them—a space that is different from what has been. A place where children are empowered to be who they are, empowered to stand up for themselves and others, and a place where they can truly discover who they are and their place in this world. This journey has come with a lot of ups and downs, mistakes, do-overs, apologies, tears, laughter, joy, sorrow—you name it! It can be difficult and lonely trying to create something new where something new has never been. It can be hard advocating for children in a way that goes against so much of what we have been taught. But I am so grateful that I have been able to experience this journey and that I have been able to do all I can to create these spaces for children. I am hopeful when I see more and more people starting to think differently about our work and about children. I hope that after reading this book, you can join me in this work of creating a collaborative educational system that values and prioritizes children above all.

I cannot believe this is my third book! It has been a lifelong dream of mine to do this and now I have done it three times! I am living proof that your dreams can come true and you can do it! It is quite a surreal experience and I would not be able to do any of this without the following people:

I first need to thank my editor Alexis and the entire team at Routledge. From the moment I met Alexis, her enthusiasm for my writing and the thoughts that I wanted to put out into the world was palpable and I could not wait to work with her. She and the entire team at Routledge have made this journey such a wonderful experience for me and I could not be more grateful. I am so glad that our paths crossed and I will forever be grateful to her for helping my dream become a reality.

To my friends who not only supported my dreams, but also spent so much of their own time reading and rereading my work, giving me suggestions, and pushing me when I felt like giving up:

Kylie, I don't know what I would do without you. Your constant support and encouragement is unmatched and I am so thankful that our paths crossed—can you believe we did it—a third time??

Ra-Sha—homie, look at this! I did it! I don't know what I would have done without you in my life all these years. I cherish our friendship and am so grateful for all you have done and continue to do for me. Look how far we have come!

Tia—my ride or die. We have long since moved beyond friends to becoming a true family. I love you so much and cannot wait to celebrate this third book with you! Love you forever.

To my girl, my sis Ron Grady—girl, I love you so much! Who would have thought that me chasing you down at a conference to meet you would have led us to where we are now! I am so thankful for you, our friendship, and where we are. Let's continue to conquer the world! Not we're legit authors and editors now girl!

To my queen, my mom Jennifer. I would not be the person I am today without you. I love you so much, and as always, this is for you!

To my boys—Oliver, Baby Bear, and Moon—daddy loves you!

To my world, my best friend, my business partner, my husband Perry. I love you more than words can express. I am so grateful to have found you and to be going on this journey of life with you by my side. There is no other way that I would have it. What team do we play for?!

And thank you to YOU! Thank you for reading this book. Thank you for doing the work. Thank you for trusting yourself. Thank you for honoring me by reading my words. You have no idea how much you mean to me.

For Product Safety Concerns and Information please contact our EU representative GPSR@taylorandfrancis.com
Taylor & Francis Verlag GmbH, Kaufingerstraße 24, 80331 München, Germany

www.ingramcontent.com/pod-product-compliance
Lightning Source LLC
Chambersburg PA
CBHW070304230426
43664CB00014B/2627